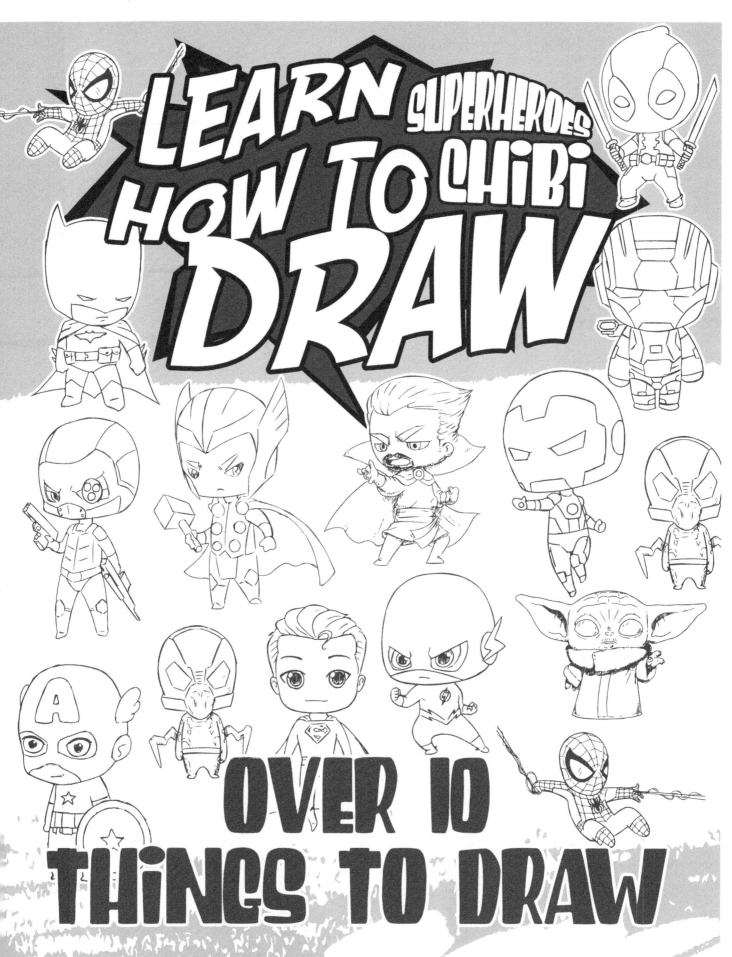

LEARN SUPERHEROES HOW TO CHIBI DRAW

OVER 10 THINGS TO DRAW

This book belong to:

TABLE OF CONTENTS

How To Use this Book

1. Draw the black lines from the first drawing.

2. Add the black lines from each additional step.

3. If you get stuck, practice by tracing the final image. Then, try drawing it yourself from the start!

You can do it!

THIS BOOK
belong to:

_____

_____

Color Chart

Chibi Yellowjacket.

1

The most noticeable feature of any chibi is their proportion, or rather the ratio of the head and body. And in the initial stage we will just mark a big rounded head and a rather small torso of chibi Yellowjacket.

2

Now, with the help of a few simple lines, we sketch the arms and legs. Note that here the proportions are also different from the proportions of an ordinary person, because the arms are noticeably longer than the legs, which is done to create a cuter appearance.

3

Now let's add some important basic details to our chibi Yellowjacket drawing using light and rough lines. Mark angular eyes, breathing apparatus and bee limbs behind the back.

Chibi Yellowjacket.

4

The rough sketch of chibi Yellowjacket is done, and starting from the fourth step we will work with clear and beautiful lines. Using such lines trace the head and mask as the Drawingforall.net artists did.

5

Now let's do the same, but with the body of our Yellowjacket. That is, trace everything using clear comic lines and remove all remaining guidelines. In the same step, draw an intricate pattern on the costume.

6

To give your Yellowjacket a more volumetric and beautiful look, you need to add some shadows. In order to do this, you need to use classic hatching and apply it on the areas indicated in the figure below.

 Chibi Yellowjacket.

YOUR TURN!!!

 Chibi Yellowjacket.

MAKE IT PERFECT!!!

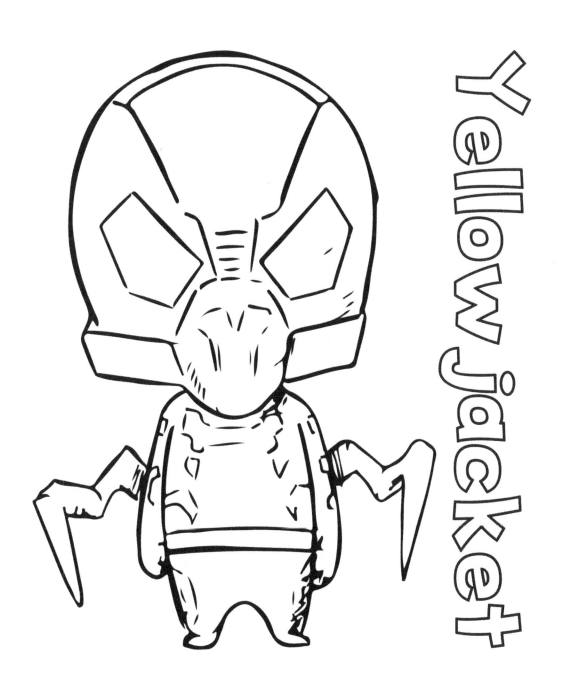

Yellow Jacket

MAKE IT PERFECT!!

 # Chibi Flash

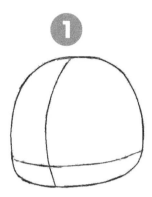

1

Let's start with the head, drawing it in the form of such a round figure. Next, draw two intersecting lines on the head.

2

Now outline the torso of chibi Flash, which is much smaller than the torso of an ordinary person.

3

Now using the horizontal line from the previous step, we draw eyes and pupils with glare inside them.

Chibi Flash

4

Carefully draw out the outlines
of the head, openings of the
mask, mouth and lightning with
the help of clear lines.

5

Now move to the torso, drawing
all outlines with the help of
clear lines. Remove unnecessary
guidelines and draw lightnings
on the suit.

 Chibi Flash

YOUR TURN!!!

 Chibi Flash

MAKE IT PERFECT!!!

Chibi Batman

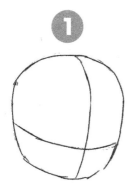

1

Like all lessons about chibi characters, our Batman begins with the outlines of a round head and intersecting lines on the head.

2

Now draw a small cartoon body of Batman. Recall that the bodies of chibi characters are very small in comparison with their heads.

3

Sketch out small pointed horns (ears) on the head, eyes, opening for the mouth and mouth itself. Next sketch out the cape and the details of the costume.

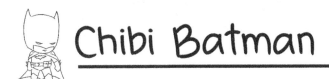

Using clear and dark lines draw out the contours of the head and remove all unnecessary guidelines.

Now go to the bottom of the body and draw out the torso, arms and legs. Draw all the details of the costume and remove all unnecessary guidelines from the chibi Batman drawing.

 ## Chibi Batman

YOUR TURN!!!

MAKE IT PERFECT!!!

MAKE IT PERFECT!!

Baby Yoda

1

First, we will draw approximate contours of the head and torso of our star baby. The head is very large, as you can see. The width and length of the head significantly exceed the size of the body. By the way, this is a pretty sure way to draw a baby.

2

Now we outline the contours of two almond-shaped eyes. Eyes should be very large, pay attention to this. The lower edge of the eyes should approximately coincide with the lower 1/3 of the face.

3

Add a small nose and mouth. The nose should be higher than the lower edge of the eyes. The mouth consists of three lines with a smooth bend.

4

What else is noteworthy in the figure and proportions of our character? Of course these are ears. Our hero has huge pointed ears that are located almost horizontally. Please note that the true Master Yoda has smaller ears.

Baby Yoda

5

This guy has really huge ears. Let's work with this feature to make the little alien more realistic. In this step we will depict the auricles. Do not forget about a couple of vertical strokes on each side

6

In this step we apply wrinkles and skin folds. As you can see, this is not a sign of old age. So, first we draw circles above and below the eyes. After that, we draw three vertical wrinkles between the eyes that look like the pattern of the Spider-Man mask. Then we add horizontal wavy lines to the forehead. At the end of the lesson, we draw small but important lines above the nose and mouth.

7

Now we outline the contours of the warm collar. Also, in this step we outline a couple of vertical lines on the body of our character.

8

Let's finish the basic body contours. To do this, we need to outline the contours of the sleeves that are trimmed with warm fur on the distal parts.

9

Remember the paws of Master Yoda? By the way, he was the greatest Jedi who masterfully owned a lightsaber. In this step we will draw the same paws with small sharp nails.

10

Let's look at our baby Yoda. We will evaluate the correct proportions and individual details. If you do not see distortions or inaccuracies, you can safely erase excess guide lines and proceed to the final steps.

11

Let's apply some shadows. You can see the shadows inside the ears of our little Yoda, under his collar and quite a bit on his face. Large shadows are best applied in two steps. First, we draw the outline of the shadow and then cover it with light shading. Very small shadows can be drawn without an outline.

12

This is the final result of our work. We hope your little Yoda looks even cooler.

Baby Yoda

YOUR TURN!!!

Baby Yoda

MAKE IT PERFECT!!!

 # Chibi Deadpool

1

2

Let's start to draw chibi Deadpool from the head. According to the tradition of drawing instructions about chibi characters, in the first step we draw a rounded head and two intersecting lines on it.

The second step of the tutorial about how to draw chibi Deadpool will also be traditional for guides about chibi - here we need to outline the torso and limbs of Deadpool. Use the most simplified lines and shapes.

3

Sketch out the eyes, katanas tight in the hands, the belt with bags and the costume lines. The initial sketch of chibi Deadpool which is the base for the future drawing is ready, and it's time to get down to the details.

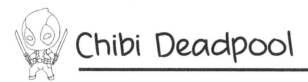

④

By clear and dark lines, carefully trace the outlines of the Deadpool's head and remove all unnecessary auxiliary lines from that cute chibi head.

⑤

Now let's deal with the body of chibi Deadpool. Draw out the lines of the costume on the chest draw details on the hands and katanas.

⑥

Draw out the belt and bags on the belt. Then draw the legs and shoes. Do not forget that since we draw a character in chibi style, there should not be too many details or little things on the artwork. The chibi Deadpool drawing is finished.

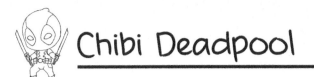

YOUR TURN!!!

MAKE IT PERFECT!!!

Chibi Captain America

1

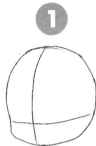

All the lessons of portrayal chibi begin with the fact that we draw their heads. In this lesson, we also first outline a rounded head and then draw two intersecting lines on it.

2

Now with the help of very light lines, we outline the disproportionately small body and the disproportionately small arms and legs of chibi Captain America.

3

Let's delineate some of the most basic details. On the head sketch the outlines of the openings of the mask, eyes, mouth and small wings. On the body we draw the outlines of the costume, a star in the center of the chest and a round shield.

4

Captain America has a staunch spirit. This is one of the most uncompromising and honest superheroes. We draw Captain America in the style of a chibi, but nevertheless we must portray his character traits in his view. Using clear and dark lines, carefully depict the eyes and glittering pupils in the eyes of our Captain America. Eyes must be resolutely frowned. Also draw the lower part of the face and mouth.

5

6

Now we will draw out the top of the head of Captain America. Carefully draw out the outlines of the head, small and cute wings on the top. At the end of the step, delete all unnecessary lines and draw the letter "A" in the center of the brow.

This step will be much easier than the rest of the lesson on how to draw Captain America. Here we carefully draw out the shape of the torso, the costume lines and the star in the core of the thorax. Do not forget to remove unnecessary lines from this area.

7

This step will be slightly more difficult than the previous one, as here will be more lines and different details. Draw a belt and small cute legs. Next, draw out the outlines of the shield and details on the shield using clear and dark lines. At the very end of the step, we simply delete all unnecessary lines.

YOUR TURN!!!

MAKE IT PERFECT!!!

Chibi Spider-Man

All the lessons of portrayal chibi begin with the fact that we draw their heads. In this lesson, we also first outline a rounded head and then draw two intersecting lines on it.

Now with the help of very light lines, we outline the disproportionately small body and the disproportionately small arms and legs of chibi Captain America.

Let's delineate some of the most basic details. On the head sketch the outlines of the openings of the mask, eyes, mouth and small wings. On the body we draw the outlines of the costume, a star in the center of the chest and a round shield.

Chibi Spider-Man

5

So we practically repeat another Spider-Man's drawing tutorial (we mean original version, not Chibi). In this step we will outline the contours of the eyes on the mask.

6

And it is practically final of the drawing tutorial in which we told and show how to draw chibi Spider-Man. In step we will make right form of the eyes. Also we will draw a web.

7

And the next step is the drawing of the web which located at the costume. In addition to the pattern of web we will also need to draw a spider's logo on the chest.

YOUR TURN!!!

MAKE IT PERFECT!!!

Chibi Iron Man

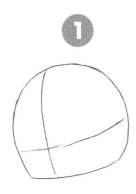

1

Like all lessons about chibi, this lesson begins with the drawing of a rounded head. After we outline the head, we need to sketch two lines of symmetry of the face.

2

Now we need to sketch the outlines of the body, arms and legs. This is very easy, since we use very light lines and simple geometric shapes.

3

Let's take care of the details. First of all we will draw out the eyes and pattern in the lower part of the head (similar to the mouth).

4

Draw out the outlines of the head with clear and dark lines. Draw the patterns as in our example and go to the next step.

Chibi Iron Man

5

Now let's move to the torso. Here we will need to draw out the outlines of the torso and patterns on the torso.

6

Now the arms. Here we draw out the outlines of the arms and details of the metal armor.

7

The same thing you need to do with the legs - that is, draw out the outlines of the legs and patterns on the legs. Try not to get lost in the details.

<u>Chibi Iron Man</u>

YOUR TURN!!!

Chibi Iron Man

MAKE IT PERFECT!!!

Iron Man

Chibi Dr. Strange

1

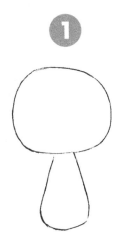

The main feature of chibi people is their unusual ratio of body parts. They have a very big head and a relatively small body. In the first step of the lesson on how to draw chibi Dr. Strange, we need to outline the head and torso.

2

The eyes of chibi persons are very large, and therefore we mark the lower line of the eyes very low. In the same stage, we sketch the center of the face by one line. In the same second step, we will need to outline the arms and legs of Dr. Strange.

3

So far, our Dr. Strange drawing looks like a simple puppet, and the task of the third step is to draw the main parts on the body. Outline the face, hair, details of the suit, including the famous cape, as well as fingers clenched in the Strange's imitative gesture.

Chibi Dr. Strange

4

The fourth step of the lesson on how to draw Dr. Strange will be devoted to the details. According to the good old tradition we start with the head, tracing the doctor's charismatic face and his hair. Clean the drawing by removing unwanted lines from the head.

5

In the fifth step of the lesson on how to draw Dr. Strange, we will draw the body. Circle the suit, long cape and wide belt. In the same step, detail the arms and legs. Completely clean the Dr. Strange drawing with the help of an eraser.

6

Shadows in comics are drawn in a certain style, and are dark and contrasting. But in this lesson we decided to make them in another version, drawing shadows with the help of a very light hatching. If your Dr. Strange drawing is similar to ours, then you did everything right.

YOUR TURN!!!

MAKE IT PERFECT!!!

Dr. Strange

Chibi Deadshot

1

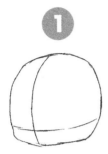

First, take a pencil in hand and sketch out the outlines of the rounded head of our chibi Deadshot. At the first step also sketch out two lines on the surface of the head.

2

Now let's deal with the body of Deadshot, outlining it in the form of a simple geometric figure. Next, in the same step, we sketch out the arms and legs.

3

Let's start to deal with the details. And by tradition, we start by draw the eyes. Note that the left eye is closed with a very cool and unusual sight.

Chibi Deadshot

4

With the help of smooth lines draw out the outlines of the head and details of the mask. Do not forget to delete all unnecessary guidelines, as shown in our example.

5

And this step will not be so simple. Here we will need to draw details of the torso and arms. Drawing these parts of the body, pay special attention to the details, trying to repeat them as in our example.

6

Also quite a difficult step. Using clear and dark lines let's draw out the outlines of the legs, also not forgetting to accurately draw the details, as shown in the example below.

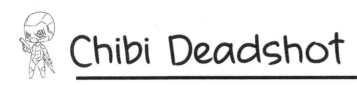

Chibi Deadshot

YOUR TURN!!!

<u>Chibi Deadshot</u>

MAKE IT PERFECT!!!

Deadshot

 # Chibi Thor

1

2

First of all sketch out the head of our chibi Thor in the form of a circle. Next, outline two intersecting lines as in our example.

Now sketch out the torso and limbs of chibi Thor with very simple geometric figures. Use almost transparent lines to map out the body of the lord of thunder and lightning.

3

4

Using light lines sketch out the helmet, eyebrows, eyes and mouth on the head. Next, sketch out the hammer in hand, the cloak and the details of the

Using clear and dark lines depict the details of the face and remove all unnecessary lines. Sketch out the eyes leaving glare in them.

Chibi Thor

5

Now trace out the outlines of the famous helmet as in the chibi Thor drawing drawn by the artists of Drawingforall.net.

6

Now let's move on to the torso and draw out all the details of the costume as in our example. Repeat the armor on the chest and mark six circles on the front of the torso.

7

Now draw out the arms, the hammer in the hand and the legs. At the end of the step draw the contours of the cape and remove all the remaining guidelines from chibi Thor drawing.

 Chibi Thor

YOUR TURN!!!

MAKE IT PERFECT!!!

Chibi Superman

1

Let's begin with the head of chibi Superman, depicting it as a circle or a rounded square. Next, draw two lines inside, as in the example from artists of Drawingforall.net.

2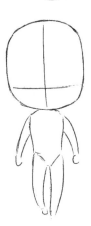

Now we move a little lower and draw out the outlines of the torso and limbs of chibi Superman. Draw them with almost transparent lines.

3

Orienting the intersecting lines on the head, draw large eyes, eyebrows and mouth. Then draw the hair and ears. Sketch out the outlines of the costume.

4

Here we will draw chibi Superman's eyes. Using dense lines draw the eye, eyebrows and nose. Paint the eyes leaving the glare inside the pupils.

Chibi Superman

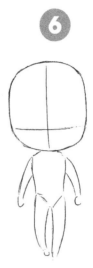

Draw the shape of the face (it should be rounded). Then draw the ears and carefully draw out the hair. The face in our chibi Superman drawing should be very sweet and cute.

Now draw the torso and hands of our chibi Superman. Depict the costume lines and draw the Superman logo on the chest.

The last step of the lesson about how to draw chibi Superman in which we draw the long cape and legs. And now it's time for an eraser, with which we will remove all the remaining unnecessary guidelines.

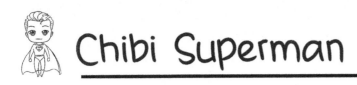

YOUR TURN!!!

YOUR TURN!!!

Chibi Superman

MAKE IT PERFECT!!!

Superman

War Machine Chibi

1

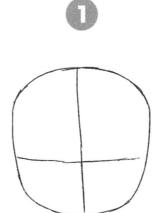

First we will draw a head. As you can see, the head is wider to the forehead and tapers to the mandible. Also, we will draw a traditional cross of the face lines. The vertical line is a line of facial symmetry. The horizontal line indicates the position of the eyes.

2

Then we will draw the body, arms and legs. Please, pay special attention to the proportions: the length of the head must be greater than the length of the torso and legs in sum.

3

Ok, it's time to sketch out eyes. After that don't forget to erase the guidelines from the previous steps to get a clean picture.

War Machine Chibi

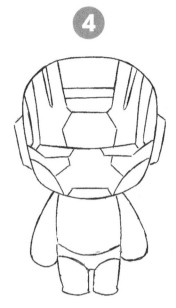

You can see so many details in this step. Draw firts the area under the eyes, and then work with the area above the eyes. This wil help you not to get confused with a lot of lines.

We come to the end of the post in which we tell you how to draw chibi War Machine. In this step we will outline the armor that covers the body.

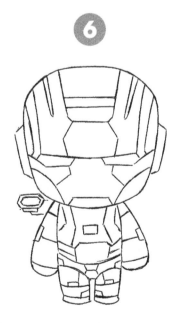

So we have a final step. Draw the armor covering the legs and arms. There is a very nice bonus of chibi drawing lessons - you don't need to draw the fingers and feet. It is a really good thing because drawing ot the palms, fists and foots - it's pretty hard problem.

YOUR TURN!!!

MAKE IT PERFECT!!!

War Machine

Made in the USA
Las Vegas, NV
11 December 2024

13868988R00063